HOUSE CLEANING

BUSINESS BLUEPRINT

The Comprehensive Guide to Start, Grow, Manage and Generate Passive Income from Cleaning

TABLE OF CONTENT

INTRODUCTION

You are about to enter the exciting world of entrepreneurship and begin the process of building a successful business from the ground up. Cleaning houses is discussed in this book as a means to a goal, one that can bring you not just financial success but also personal fulfillment.

As was previously indicated, the unending demand for home and commercial cleaning services presents an incredible opportunity for entrepreneurs. I hope this guidance can alter your perspective and help you succeed financially in this industry.

Since there is always a need for cleaning services, starting a cleaning business can be very profitable. In addition to the obvious demand in the market, cleaning businesses also have other advantages, such as a low barrier to entry, low startup costs, and low overhead compared to other business types.

You are ready to delve into the arena of business success when you have the required licenses and insurance, a minimal stockpile of cleaning products, a simple marketing plan, and steadfast dedication. This book will walk you through every step of starting your own cleaning company from scratch.

CHAPTER ONE

THE CLEANING INDUSTRY

The Demand for Cleanliness and Convenience

The need for in-home support services has skyrocketed in the modern day, when time is of the essence and maintaining a healthy work-life balance is a daily uphill battle. Due to the hectic pace of modern life, many people find it difficult to devote the time and energy required to keep their homes in the condition in which they would like to keep them. This has led to a meteoric rise in demand for expert residential cleaning services.

A large cross-section of consumers make up the target audience for this rising demand. People from many walks of life, from those with full schedules to those supporting multi-income families, seek out the convenience and cleanliness provided by a professional cleaning service. The appeal isn't simply in getting rid of a home duty; it's also in giving a helpful service that fits in with today's way of life.

As the demand for efficient methods of saving time increases, the value of professional house cleaning services as a means of enhancing people's daily lives continues to rise.

Low Entry Barriers and High Potential Profits

In contrast to other industries, the house cleaning business can be easily entered by someone with less than stellar financial wherewithal. If you have the necessary knowledge and are willing to take some risks, you may launch a successful cleaning business with little to no initial investment. Congratulations, you've just guaranteed yourself a steady stream of money for the rest of your life.

Keep in mind that this sector's unique selling point sets it apart from other business spheres, making it a practical choice for aspiring business owners on a tight budget. When broken down, the house cleaning company concept not only provides a low-barrier-to-entry but also tremendous profit potential.

Building recurring service agreements and making sure that clients are satisfied are vital since they help to create a continuous and long-lasting cash stream. The cleaning business's long-term sustainability and financial viability improves when new, repeat customers are added to the roster of satisfied regulars.

The house cleaning sector, in essence, offers a low-barrier-to-entry and the chance to start and expand a profitable business with little to no initial expenditure. The potential for steady profit increases the attractiveness of entering this industry and demonstrates how an entrepreneurial activity in this area can grow into a successful and long-lasting enterprise.

Flexibility and Independence

I take it you've already decided that starting a house cleaning business is the way to go if you're the independent, self-starting sort that values freedom and independence above all else. So let proceed.

This type of business ownership affords you the rare opportunity to not only choose your own schedule, but also to carefully choose your clients and direct the development of your company in the direction that best suits your goals.

House cleaning services are appealing because they may be tailored to meet a wide variety of customer needs. The unique freedom and independence inherent to this profession provide a vast canvas for your entrepreneurial goals, whether you're looking to supplement your current income, make a smooth transfer from a conventional career, or grow a successful firm.

The freedom to design a business around your needs and goals means you can choose your own hours, work with clients that share your beliefs, and control how quickly you grow. Those who want for independence and a sense of agency in their professional lives may find the house cleaning business to be an attractive option because to its financial potential and the opportunities it provides for personal growth and development.

An Industry with Integrity

Trust, integrity, and an unyielding dedication to providing exceptional service are the bedrock upon which the house cleaning industry rests. When you enter this exciting sector, you'll be responsible for protecting people's most prized possessions—their houses. Relationships with customers are more than just a means to a goal; they're also testimonials to your company's commitment to providing people with pleasant, healthy places to live.

As I travel farther in the pages of this book, I am set to transmit a wealth of knowledge, insights, and methods that have the transformational capacity to metamorphosis your goals of running a house cleaning company into a flourishing reality. The investigation will be all-encompassing, covering every part of the company from its inception to its intricate marketing strategies, day-to-day operations, and future expansion plans.

After reading this book, you'll be ready to start your own cleaning firm and take the plunge into the exciting world of entrepreneurship as you work tirelessly for that all-important first paycheck. Consider this your first step toward being a successful house cleaner if you are ready to embark on this exciting adventure. Open the book and join me on a life-altering adventure.

CHAPTER TWO

THE BLUEPRINT

"A solid blueprint tells you what? You know what you are doing"

Administrative "To Do's"

Establishing a house cleaning company requires meeting a number of legal and administrative requirements, such as acquiring the necessary licenses and registering the firm with the appropriate authorities. These procedural components hold essential relevance in insuring the lawful running of your organization and generating a sense of trust and confidence among potential clients. In order to ensure the success of your cleaning company, you must invest significant time and energy into building a solid foundation.

When building trust with customers, it's important to remember that strict adherence to legal and regulatory regulations is more important than cutting corners on administrative work and saving money.

Putting your company's legitimacy first is a certain way to win over skeptical clients.

Building a Business Structure and Name

Making an educated choice on the legal structure of your company is an important first step in launching a house cleaning service before diving into the processes of licensing and registration. There are a few different legal structures that can be used to organize a business; they include the sole proprietorship, partnership, limited liability company (LLC), and corporation. Your business's fundamental framework will be heavily influenced by the legal form you choose.

Once you have settled on a legal structure for your house cleaning service, the next step is to think of and settle on a suitable name for your venture. This nomenclature not only acts as the identification of your business but also plays a key function in developing a unique market presence. The possibility for legal issues increases dramatically if the chosen name is already in use by another business in your area.

A quick and thorough search of the company registry in your state should reveal whether or not the name you've picked is already in use. This preventative action places your house cleaning company on a firm and lawful footing by protecting your brand identification and ensuring compliance with legal requirements.

Steps to follow in Registering Your Business

Pick a location for your company's headquarters. This might be a storefront or your spare bedroom. When deciding where to set your shop, be sure to take zoning regulations into account.

Your business should be registered with the appropriate state and municipal agencies. This usually entails submitting the required paperwork and paying the associated registration charge. Get in touch with the office of the Secretary of State or the county clerk in your area to get the specifics.

Opening a business bank account and filing taxes both require a valid Employer Identification Number (EIN), also called a Federal Tax Identification

Number. You can apply for an EIN with the Internal Revenue Service (IRS) either online or by mail.

To find out if your house cleaning service needs any special licenses or permits, contact the appropriate authorities in your area. There are a variety of licenses and permits that may be required before starting a home-based business.

You will require a sales tax license if your state charges sales tax on cleaning services. The ability to charge and collect sales tax on services is a result of this.

After obtaining the required state licenses and permits for your cleaning business, the next step is to stock up on the tools and materials you'll need to get started. Knowing what tools and materials will be necessary on your path to building a successful house cleaning business is crucial. The tools at your disposal have a significant impact on the quality of your job, the happiness of your customers, and the efficacy of your business.

CLEANING TOOLS AND EQUIPMENT

"The quality and reliability of your equipment and supplies directly impact the quality of your service and your clients' satisfaction"

Vacuum Cleaners

Invest in high-quality vacuum cleaners equipped with HEPA filters. These are essential for thorough carpet and floor cleaning.

Mops and Brooms

Quality mops and brooms are indispensable for maintaining clean and polished floors. Microfiber mops are efficient for removing dust and dirt.

Cleaning Cloths and Microfiber Towels

These versatile items are used for various cleaning tasks, from dusting to wiping surfaces. Microfiber cloths are particularly effective at trapping dirt and germs.

- ### Sponges and Scrubbing Pads

Sponges and scrubbing pads are essential for tackling tougher cleaning tasks, such as scrubbing grime from sinks and countertops.

Buckets and Caddies

Durable cleaning buckets and caddies keep your tools organized and transport cleaning supplies efficiently from room to room.

Trash Bags

High-quality trash bags are essential for collecting and disposing of waste during cleaning.

Dusters and Dusting Tools

A variety of dusters, including feather dusters and extendable dusters, are crucial for dusting surfaces, light fixtures, and hard-to-reach areas.

Window Cleaning Tools

Squeegees, window scrubbers, and extension poles are vital for achieving streak-free, crystal-clear windows.

Cleaning Caddies

These handy containers allow you to organize and carry cleaning supplies efficiently.

Floor Cleaning Machines

For larger operations, investing in floor scrubbers and polishers can significantly reduce cleaning time and enhance the quality of your services.

High-Quality Cleaning Products

All-Purpose Cleaners: Versatile and essential for cleaning various surfaces throughout the home, including kitchens and bathrooms.

Disinfectants and Sanitizers: Especially important in the current climate, these products help eliminate germs and create a healthier living environment.

Glass Cleaners: Ensure your glass cleaner leaves surfaces streak-free and crystal clear.

Bathroom Cleaners: Effective products for removing soap scum, mold, and mildew in bathrooms.

Kitchen Cleaners: These products are designed to tackle grease, grime, and food-related stains.

Floor Cleaners: Use floor-specific cleaners for different types of flooring, such as hardwood, tile, or laminate.

Specialty Cleaners: Invest in specialty cleaners for stainless steel, granite, and other unique surfaces you may encounter.

Oven and Stovetop Cleaners: Powerful cleaners to remove baked-on stains and grease from ovens and stovetops.

Furniture Polishes: High-quality furniture polishes are essential for wood and leather surfaces.

- Safety Gear and Accessories
- Gloves: Protect your hands from chemicals and allergens with high-quality cleaning gloves.
- Face Masks: Especially crucial when dealing with allergens or airborne particles.

- Protective Eyewear: Guard your eyes against splashes and debris when working with cleaning agents.

- Aprons and Protective Clothing: Durable aprons and clothing protect your attire from stains and spills.

- Shoe Covers: These help prevent dirt and contaminants from being tracked into homes.

Remember, invest in high-quality products and maintain them meticulously to ensure your cleaning business not only meets but exceeds your clients' expectations.

PRICING AND SERVICES

The term "price" refers to the agreed-upon and actual monetary exchange for a given commodity or service. In addition to its monetary meaning, pricing can be seen as the cost that buyers must bear in order to enjoy the benefits of an item.

To put it simply, price is a vital component of the marketing mix, differing from the other aspects like product, promotion, and place which are usually more expensive. Conversely, price is the factor that has the most impact on whether or not a product or service generates income.

In addition, pricing becomes a strategic component of the company environment, serving as an effective instrument for generating consumer value. The goal of any pricing strategy should be to maximize profits while still satisfying customers. Market dynamics and consumer behavior are heavily influenced by this intricate interplay.

Pricing Strategies

Customer-Based Pricing

The principle behind customer value-based pricing is to price a product based on the value it provides to customers rather than the cost of production; thus, the pricing decision begins with assessing customer value - how much the product is worth to customers. Within value-based pricing, there are two further pricing approaches; Good-value pricing and Value-based pricing.

Good-value pricing involves offering a quality product and good service at a reasonable price while value-based pricing includes adding value through product features and services to justify the higher prices.

Cost-Based Pricing

Cost-based pricing is the second most common pricing technique. Cost-based pricing entails setting prices based on the costs of manufacturing and marketing the goods. This pricing strategy establishes a floor price, or the lowest price a corporation should charge to recover costs. This approach considers three sorts of costs

- Fixed expenses (overhead)
- Variable expenses
- Total expenses

One common cost-based pricing method is cost-plus pricing. Cost-plus pricing involves adding a pre-set mark-up to the cost of producing a product (e.g. adding a 20% mark-up). Another approach to cost-based pricing is break-even pricing.

This pricing method is based on finding the break-even point whereby the firm recovers all production and marketing costs.

Competition-Based Pricing

The final primary pricing strategy is competition-based pricing. Competition-based pricing involves setting prices based on competitors' pricing strategies. To use this approach, you need to examine your competitors and their strategies, including:

- Competitors' market offering
- Customers' value perception of competitors' offerings
- Competitors' current pricing strategies,
- How strong/weak competitors are
- Whether there is a niche/underserved market.

Pricing Your Cleaning Service

Setting the right prices for your cleaning services is a delicate balance that can significantly impact the success of your house cleaning company.

Pricing your cleaning services should be a well-thought-out process that takes various factors into account. Some of which are;

Cost of Operations

Calculate the expenses associated with running your business, including labor, supplies, equipment, and overhead. This serves as the foundation for your pricing structure.

Service Complexity

Different cleaning tasks require varying levels of effort and time. Price your services accordingly, considering the intricacy of the job.

Location and Demographics

Take into account the location of your clients and their demographics. High-end neighborhoods may support higher prices, while lower-income areas might require more competitive rates.

Profit Margin

Ensure your pricing allows for a healthy profit margin while remaining competitive. A typical rule of thumb is to aim for a 10-30% profit margin.

Customization

Offer flexibility for customizing services. Some clients may require additional tasks or have specific preferences, which can justify higher pricing.

Discounts and Promotions

Strategically use discounts and promotions, such as first-time client discounts or seasonal offers, to attract new clients.

CHAPTER THREE

MARKETING AND BRANDING

The term "marketing" is used to describe an organization's broad range of efforts to increase demand for a given product or service. Marketing, sales, and trouble-free product distribution are just a few examples of the many components that fall under this umbrella. It is important to note that a company's affiliates may also engage in marketing on its behalf, thereby expanding the reach and impact of the campaign.

Seth Godin, a prominent figure in the marketing realm, aptly captures the multifaceted nature of marketing by describing it as the comprehensive act of inventing a product, the dedicated effort in designing it, the skilled craft involved in its production, the artistry embedded in pricing strategies, and the nuanced technique applied in selling it to the target audience.

The "Four Ps" are product, price, location, and promotion form the basis of a marketing strategy. Individually or in combination, these Four Ps form the backbone of any successful marketing strategy. Neil Borden first introduced the notion of the marketing mix and the Four Ps in the 1950s, and they continue to play a central role in assisting firms in developing and implementing successful marketing strategies.

Product

A product is an item or goods that a company intends to sell to clients. The goal of the product should be to fill a need in the market or to satisfy a consumer need for a greater quantity of an existing product. In order to create a successful marketing strategy, you must have a thorough understanding of the product being sold, including how it compares to similar products on the market, whether it can be used in conjunction with other products, and whether there are any available alternatives.

Price

The price of a product is determined by the company. When setting a price, you have to take into account distribution costs, marketing costs, and unit cost pricing. Also, have a look at how your competitors are pricing their items and see if the savings they claim to offer is enough to sway consumer opinion.

Place

The dispersion of the product is referred to as its location. Key factors include whether the product will be offered in a physical location, online, or through both channels. When it's sold in a physical store, what kind of promotion does it receive? When it's bought and sold online, does it get any sort of digital product placement?

Promotion

Promotion, the fourth P, is the integrated marketing communications campaign. Promotion involves a variety of activities such as advertising, selling, sales promotions, public relations, direct marketing, sponsorship, and guerilla marketing. Marketing campaigns change as the product progresses through its life cycle. Keep in mind that buyers will factor in the product's price and distribution into their overall marketing strategy evaluation of the product's quality..

Branding Your Cleaning Business

Branding is an important component of your cleaning company that extends far beyond a logo or a catchy slogan. It includes developing and managing your company's image, reputation, and the emotions it generates in your customers. Branding is the process of building a distinct identity for your cleaning company. It is how you distinguish your firm from competitors and establish a strong, recognizable presence in the minds of your clientele. Effective branding not only fosters trust and loyalty, but it also encourages potential clients to choose your services over others.

The following are key elements for branding of a cleaning business;

Business Name

Your business name is often the first point of contact with potential clients. It should be memorable, easy to spell, and reflective of your services. Ensure it's not already in use in your area and consider securing a domain name for your website.

Logo and Visual Identity

A well-designed logo and consistent visual elements, such as color schemes and fonts, create a strong visual identity for your business. Your logo should be professional and memorable, reflecting the qualities you want your brand to embody.

Mission and Values

Clearly define your company's mission and core values. What do you stand for, and what kind of service can clients expect from you? This should be reflected in your marketing materials and on your website.

Professional Website

In the digital age, a professional website is a non-negotiable element of your branding. Your website should be user-friendly, mobile-responsive, and provide essential information about your services, pricing, and contact details.

Tagline

A short and memorable tagline can reinforce your brand message and values. It should encapsulate the essence of your cleaning business in a few words.

Professionalism

Everything about your business, from the appearance of your staff to the cleanliness of your equipment and vehicles, should exude professionalism. This is a crucial aspect of branding as it directly impacts clients' perception of your company.

Website Development

You can't build any kind of credible online reputation without a quality website. It's the initial impression you make on potential customers, so it should inspire confidence in your abilities and enthusiasm for working with you. A lot of the cleaning companies out there don't even have a website. Companies serving a wide geographic area or numerous states are more likely to have a website than their smaller counterparts. This is because the cost of establishing up a website and maintaining it does not seem to be worth the rewards.

The majority of similar cleaning services exclusively advertise via traditional and online channels. While any advertising is preferable to none, many company owners fail to consider the website's long-term benefits. Here are some reasons why you might want to create a website.

First, I'll explain the advantages, and then you may decide whether or not a website is necessary for your cleaning company. After that, I'll show you how to increase your website's potential for generating leads.

Website Legitimizes Your Business

According to Social Media Today, a website is one of the four ways to make your business look legitimate. What this means is that once a potential client takes a look at your website, there will already be a higher form of trust established. This trust would not exist if you only worked through a Facebook page. Just imagine, you find two businesses that are equal on every footing. However, one of them has a professional website, and the other one just a Facebook page. Which one are you more likely to retain?

Websites Allow Organic Marketing

A lot of small businesses do not understand the effectiveness of organic marketing. Even something as simple as a blog can have huge benefits. Organic marketing is a low-cost strategy that may not be as effective as traditional marketing channels in the short run but will benefit your cleaning business immensely within a few months. A website will also help you get new clients through Search Engine Optimization.

Of course, it is possible for you to hire a professional service for SEO purposes. In fact, it is possible to outsource your entire marketing if you are serious about growth. However, those just starting out or those on a shoestring budget can actually do basic SEO themselves.

Provide Valuable Information

Social media platforms are great. They allow you to regularly interact with your customers and provide an insight into the world of cleaning. However, social media platforms are designed to display the most recent posts, photos, and videos. As such, the explainer videos that you made at the start will probably be lost in the noise. A website can be a great way to display information that lets the visitor know what your cleaning business does, and how your services can be utilized. A contact page or a form can be the difference between signing a new client or losing one to someone that has a clear procedure for hiring them.

Convert

Lastly, you can direct your ads to a specific landing page. Whereas ads (regardless of where they are) are meant to be attention grabbers and provide a quick blurb about your business, a landing page is meant to convert. A landing page can have all the details that are important to a potential client. At the end, you can guide the visitor on how to contact you.

Have I been able to convince you? While it may seem like a hassle, a website could be the main thing missing from your marketing strategy. A professionally built website could very well be what separates you from your competition.

CHAPTER FOUR

HIRING AND MANAGING STAFF FOR YOUR CLEANING BUSINESS

You have done well to get your cleaning business up and running, considering all the challenges you faced. Your efforts have not only laid the framework for the success of your firm, but have also contributed to its expansion and increased patronage. Your determination to find the optimal pricing point for your cleaning services is more evidence of your commitment to smart business methods.

Now that your cleaning firm has grown to the point that you can't handle all of the work on your own, you'll need to consider investing in better supplies and maybe even adding staff in the form of a cleaning crew. However, at this moment, there arise a number of issues that may appear insurmountable.

The topic of how to begin the process of enhancing your cleaning supplies and expanding your workforce emerges. It can be difficult to understand how to give someone else the responsibility of living up to your high standards. There are a number of factors to think about as you make your way through this change. How do you even begin to get dependable cleaning supplies? How do you screen candidates to find those who can deliver the results your clients have grown to expect? What is the best way to get the word out about a job vacancy so that competent people apply?

If any of these things are bothering you, know that you are not alone. Many entrepreneurs confront similar challenges when they expand their businesses. The key is to take a deliberate and strategic approach to every detail, from researching and selecting high-quality cleaning products to developing a solid hiring plan in line with the company's principles.

Traits to Look for When Hiring Cleaning Staff

First of all, you need to figure out what kind of employee you want. If you don't know what you want before you start writing a job ad, you will be hiring the right people. Take into consideration what makes you good at what you do: friendliness, trustworthiness, experience, and hard work.

Here are some of the most important traits to look for when hiring cleaning staff:

- Friendliness: If they come into contact with your clients, you want to know that they are friendly and will not scare away the clients.

- Trustworthiness: Clients are entrusting you with their comfort zone. They will have a variety of items they consider valuable. You will want to know that you can trust anyone you send into someone else's place. Depending upon your clientele, you may even want to conduct a criminal background check.

- Previous cleaning experience: Working for a cleaning company is hard and intensive labor. Hiring cleaners with previous cleaning experience will ensure they know what is required of them. You can also consider people that have experience in any physically demanding job.

- Ability to solve problems: Chances are, even if there is a team in one location, each employee will have to work independently to cover more ground. Each employee should be independent and self-motivated enough to be able to solve minor issues without always finding someone else to do it. Problem-solving skills keep work flowing.

- Dedication: You need a team that will be there when scheduled, instead of continually calling off work or sweeping things under a rug (sometimes literally!).

The Hiring Process

Hiring is an important step in selecting the proper individuals for your cleaning company. This procedure can take some time because there are multiple phases involved, including examining applications, phoning people, doing interviews, conducting background checks and reference checks, possibly conducting a second interview, and negotiating a salary.

Before you begin, make sure you have estimated your payroll budget so you know what you can afford.

Step 1 – Review Applications

It is possible to receive so many applications that you can't read them all. It is recommended to set a specific time period for application submissions (like 30 days). However too short of a time frame may not get you many applications, while too long of a time frame can force people to move on to other potential jobs.

Once you start receiving them, sort through all the applications and arrange them in order of very interested, somewhat interested, and not-at-all pile. From there, you can move on to the next step.

Step 2 – Set up Initial Interviews or Screening

As part of your cleaning staffing process, you can conduct a quick phone interview as an initial screening. Ask the person if now is a good time for an initial phone interview, or if they have a preferred date and time. A quick discussion can give you an idea of what kind of employee they would be.

Step 3 – The Interview

The in-person interview can tell you a lot about an applicant's personality. It also gives the person a chance to discuss their strengths and background. Determine what questions you want to ask before your first interview.

Questions can be about anything from previous jobs they've held, why they are interested in working for you, and where they see themselves in a couple of years. But be careful not to ask illegal questions, such as age and religious preference.

Step 4 – Background Checks

Once you have picked out a few candidates, you can have some background checks conducted to find out about any criminal offenses. The candidates have to give their consent to perform this, but it is a form easily found online. Most background-checking websites will charge a fee for this service.

Step 5 – Check References

Checking references can provide you with information on what other people and previous bosses think of the candidate. While it is possible to receive only references that the candidate knows will give a useful review, they are still worth checking.

Optional Step – Second Interview

A second interview is not always necessary, but it can help you determine who you like best out of all the candidates who have made it this far. You can also ask other questions that you didn't think to ask in the first interview.

Step 6 – Job Offer

By this point, you should already know what you are willing to pay your employees and if you are going to offer benefits. While some people will take the offer as given, some will want to negotiate. Do not go outside of your budget for what you can afford. You can also set up a probationary period and give your new employee a raise if they meet your expectations.

EMPLOYEE MANAGEMENT

Reasons Why Employees Stay

Reduce turnover by learning the factors that make workers content and invested in their work. This expertise can help you save time and money for your firm. Money is rarely the primary reason given by those leaving their careers. Now is the time to offer health insurance to employees if you haven't already. People who have health insurance are very serious about seeking for jobs. Numerous insurance companies exist to aid firms of any size in locating cost-effective protection. Individuals value and will work hard to maintain other benefits such as paid sick leave and paid vacation time.

Both the business and its workers will reap the rewards of a positive work environment. A positive corporate culture can be fostered in part by adopting a philosophy that promotes the kind of healthy and stimulating workplace atmosphere you seek.

Superb managers inspire their staff to do their best. Think back on your time at your most recent fantastic employment. That person was lovely to be around in addition to supporting you and acknowledging your accomplishments. They inspired you to put in long hours and have fun at work.

Hiring the right people is like putting money into the future of your company. If workers don't believe they are contributing to the company's success, they won't be invested in their jobs. Workers will become more committed to the company if they feel valued and appreciated.

Reasons Why Employees Leave

Just as important as learning what causes people to leave is discovering what keeps them there. You may be able to influence some of these factors, but others, such as an employee's private life, are outside of your sphere of influence.

If you don't have faith in your employees, they will notice. If an employee has doubts about your confidence in them, they may start to question why you hired them. The same is true of the experience of being unappreciated. Appreciation for a job well done is greatly appreciated.

They will see that you don't trust their judgment or value them if you micromanage them.

Not only will employees leave a bad boss, but so will potential consumers. Consider the worst manager you've ever worked for. Consider how you felt as a result of their actions. You ended up hating that person, and that job, didn't you? How did that awful manager make you feel about the organization overall?

Employees may leave a company if they are not offered health insurance or other advantages. Providing health insurance to your staff is a win-win situation, since they will be healthier and miss less work as a result.

FINANCIAL MANAGEMENT FOR YOUR CLEANING BUSINESS

A cleaning company's success and long-term viability are largely dependent on the establishment and upkeep of sound financial management procedures. I will examine the subtle nuances involved in developing reliable bookkeeping and accounting systems throughout our investigation. I will also examine the skill of skillfully handling spending and negotiating the nuances of tax obligations. A thorough comprehension of these financial aspects is crucial for your company's stability as well as for accelerating growth and streamlining strategic decision-making.

The careful implementation of sound financial practices is pivotal in steering your cleaning business through the intricacies of financial management. By putting in place meticulous accounting and bookkeeping systems, you not only enhance the transparency of your financial transactions but also cultivate a structured approach to monitoring and analyzing your fiscal health.

Keeping costs under control and figuring out the complex tax laws both add to the financial stability of your cleaning business. In addition to ensuring compliance, wise resource management and strict adherence to tax laws also strategically place your company in the highly competitive market.

Acknowledging the importance of financial reporting also becomes apparent as a vital tool in the financial management toolbox. Not only can accurate and timely financial reports give you valuable information about your cleaning company's financial performance, but they can also enable you to make well-informed and strategic decisions that will help your business grow steadily.

Setting up Accounting and Bookkeeping

Accounting is the process of recording a company's financial transactions. This comprises summarizing, analyzing, and reporting on business income and expenses to regulatory agencies, tax collectors, and business partners or investors. This entails keeping track of your transactions and making sure you're meeting all of your tax requirements.

You must be aware of how to manage your company's finances and cash flow. This will allow you to make more informed financial decisions, manage your expenses, and prevent costly tax blunders.

1. File a Cleaning Service Registration Form with the State

The first step that every cleaning service owners must take before opening their doors is to set up shop. The first step is to choose a business structure. Many small business entrepreneurs begin as sole proprietorships. This indicates that the company is not a separate legal entity and does not submit separate business tax filings. A sole proprietorship is the simplest business structure, but it also means you might be held personally liable for the company's debts or responsibilities. Consider forming a limited liability company (LLC) to isolate your business finances from your personal finances. You don't have to file a separate tax return for your business as a single-member LLC. Whatever business structure you choose for your small business, you need to apply for an employer identification number (EIN).

This is an eight-digit number that acts as a tax identification number for small businesses. You can apply for an EIN online for free, and it takes just a few minutes. Most banks require an EIN to set up checking accounts for small businesses.

2. Set up a Business Bank Account

The first step in organizing your business financials is to separate your personal accounts from your business accounts. You should open at least one separate business bank account for your cleaning business. Make sure all of your cleaning business income gets deposited into your business checking account and that all business expenses run through the business account instead of your personal account. You can also pay your business taxes out of the business bank account.

Don't charge any personal expenses to your business account. Instead, pay yourself a draw and use that money to cover personal expenses. This will make your bookkeeping much cleaner and make it easier to estimate your taxes.

You can open business bank accounts at your local bank or credit union, or an online bank. Simply go to your preferred bank or credit union to discuss your options for a new business checking account. In order to set up a business bank account for your cleaning business, you will need:

- Social security number or employer identification number (EIN)
- Form of personal identification, such as driver's license or passport
- Business license with the name of your cleaning business
- Organizing documents filed with the state
- Monthly credit card revenue (for merchant accounts)

3. Create a Cleaning Log

Next, you will want to create a cleaning log in order to keep track of your clients and the revenue coming in. This log will also help you see how long it takes to clean a home or office so you can monitor the financial health of your business, such as determining whether you need to raise your prices for services, speed up your cleaning time, or both.

Your cleaning log should include:

- Date
- Clients' names
- Start time and end time
- Total cleaning fee for the cleaning service
- Labor costs and expenses.

4. Save Your Receipts

Cleaning businesses typically have low overhead costs, but it's still important to keep track of your expenses so you are not only aware of how much money is coming in, but how much money is going out.

These expenses can sneak up on you using an expense tracker or bookkeeping software and saving your receipts can help you avoid slipping into "the red," i.e., losing money. Take note of how much you spend on cleaning supplies, cleaning tools, payroll, office supplies, marketing and advertising, professional services, equipment, transportation.

5. Track Business Miles

Small cleaning business owners spend a lot of time traveling between clients' houses or offices, and you can claim a tax deduction for those miles. There are two ways to deduct vehicle expenses: you can use the standard mileage method or the actual expenses method.

Whichever method you use, you need to track how many miles you drive for your cleaning business versus how many miles you drive for personal purposes. You can do this with a mileage log kept in your glove compartment or using technology.

Many popular accounting software programs, including FreshBooks, feature built-in mileage tracking in the mobile app. All you need to do is note your beginning and ending mileage for the year, then classify each trip in the app as either business or personal.

6. Invest in Online Accounting Software

While manual bookkeeping methods like a spreadsheet program or PDF invoice templates exist to help you keep your business finances organized, they can only take you so far. As your small cleaning business grows, you'll need a more powerful solution to help you manage many cleaning jobs at once.

That's where automated accounting software comes in. With an online solution, you can invoice clients for services in a matter of minutes, get paid faster, and manage all of your small business accounting in one place. You can also generate reports and get a better idea of what to set aside for tax season.

7. Reconcile Your Transactions

Every month your bank will send you a statement that includes your deposits and withdrawals (income and expenses, respectively) that went through your business account. With this information, you will want to reconcile all of the transactions on this statement with the transactions recorded in your accounting software.

You need to keep a record of all transactions so managing their small business bookkeeping (not to mention tax time) is hassle-free.

Reconciling your transactions involves:

- Comparing your bank records to your receipts
- Looking for any discrepancies
- Calculating total revenue and expenses
- Comparing any transactions to what you have in your expense of revenue sheets
- Contacting your bank and/or accountant to discuss any errors

If you use accounting software, it's easy to connect the accounting software to your business bank accounts. Any transactions that run through your bank account will be automatically recorded in your books, which makes reconciling the bank account quick and easy.

8. Pay Estimated Quarterly Taxes

As a cleaning business owner, you pay taxes throughout the year rather than paying a bill tax bill when you file your tax return. Paying quarterly taxes will not only give you peace of mind knowing your tax liability is covered, but will help you avoid any costly surprises at the end of the year that might interrupt your cash flow.

Owning a successful cleaning service requires that you stay on top of your bookkeeping and keep track of all your income tax information. Remember, you not only need to pay income taxes. As the owner of a business in the cleaning industry, you're self-employed, so you need to pay self-employment taxes as well.

To pay estimated quarterly taxes, you have a few options, including:

- Signing up for the Electronic Federal Tax Payment System (EFTPS) online
- Paying online via the IRS website
- Paying using debit or credit card
- Sending a check or money order by mail to the IRS

9. Hire an Accountant (Optional)

It's entirely possible to manage your cleaning business accounting on your own with the help of accounting software, but it's easier when you have a professional accountant on your side. An accountant will help you make sense of the numbers, reconcile your accounts, prepare financial reports, estimate your quarterly tax payments, and more.

CONCLUSION

This book is a comprehensive guide to starting and growing a successful house cleaning business. I will show you everything you need to know, from coming up with a business idea to handling finances and expanding your business.

This journey has taught you the importance of professionalism, dependability, and customer satisfaction in building a stellar reputation for your cleaning business. You've mastered the art of marketing your services to the masses, and as a result, your company is now a household name.

This book has provided you the tools you need to put up a sound accounting system that will serve as the cornerstone of your financial success. In order to keep your business afloat, you've studied budgeting, spending analysis, and tax management.

Keep in mind that the cleaning industry is about more than just tidying up; it's about making a difference in people's lives. With hard work, careful attention to detail, and the knowledge you'll get from this manual, your cleaning business can rise above the competition, realize your entrepreneurial dreams, and make houses shine for one client at a time.

Achieving your goals in the cleaning business is not out of reach. Take advantage of this expanding industry by putting the advice you've just read into practice and building a successful cleaning business. The potential outcomes of your voyage are vast. I hope that your cleaning business thrives and grows to become as spotless as the homes it maintains.